SPANISH

Colophon

© 2003 Rebo International b.v., Lisse, The Netherlands

www.rebo-publishers.com – info@rebo-publishers.com

This 2nd edition reprinted 2004

Original recipes and photographs: © R&R Publishing Pty. Ltd.

Design, editing, production and layout: Minkowsky Graphics, Enkhuizen, The Netherlands

Translation and adaptation: American Pie, London, UK and Sunnyvale, California, USA

ISBN 90 366 1480 5

SPANISH

bring sunny Spain into your kitchen with

creative cooking

REBO
PUBLISHERS

Foreword

Whether Spain reminds you of Flamenco dancers, summer love affairs

on white, sandy beaches, or Antonio Gaudí, all involve passion, as

does Spanish cuisine, which has many secrets besides the familiar

Paella and Tapas, secrets that are full of passion. If you put on a frilly,

red dress and black mantilla, I will fill the glasses with Sangrìa.

The dishes selected for this book originate from all over Spain, from

the coasts—Fish Soup with Saffron, Fried Sea-bream—to the

interior—Artichokes Braised in White Wine, Boiled Beef Madrid-style,

and Bean Casserole with Chorizo.

You look fantastic, may I have the pleasure of this pasa doble with

you? Then we will choose a dessert.

Abbreviations

tbsp = tablespoon

tsp = teaspoon

g = gram

kg = kilogram

fl oz = fluid ounce

lb = pound

oz = ounce

ml = milliliter

l = liter

°C = degree Celsius

°F = degree Fahrenheit

Where three measurements are given,

the first is the American liquid measure.

Method

Combine all the ingredients, except the chicken, avocado, and lettuce, in a food processor and process until smooth. Refrigerate this dressing for at least one hour for the flavors to mingle.

When ready to serve, arrange the shredded lettuce on plates, top with the cubed chicken and avocado and spoon the dressing over them.

Ingredients

2 cups/1lb/450g cooked cubed chicken

8 anchovy fillets, soaked in milk, rinsed and dried

1 small red Bermuda onion, minced

2 tbsp/50g chopped fresh tarragon

2 tbsp/50g chopped fresh chives

4 tbsp/100g minced fresh parsley

1¼ cups/9½ fl oz/280ml fresh mayonnaise

Chicken and Avocado Salad

⅔ cup/5 fl oz/140ml plain yogurt

2 tbsp tarragon vinegar

pinch of hot chili pepper or paprika

pinch of sugar

1 romaine lettuce, shredded

1 ripe avocado, cubed

Spanish

Method

1.- Preheat the oven to 350°F/180°C. Spread the almonds on a cookie sheet and toast for about 20 minutes, until fragrant and golden.

2.- Ad the salt to the egg white. Add the almonds and shake well to coat

3.- Tip the almonds out on to the cookie sheet, shake it to spread the nuts apart, then return them to the oven for 5 minutes, until they have dried. Leave until cold, then store in an airtight container until ready to serve.

Salted Almonds

Tip

You can also use blanched almonds or blanch the almonds before toasting. Other flavorings can be added to the salt, such as ground pepper and cumin.

Ingredients

½ tsp/2.5g coarse sea salt

1 tbsp/15 ml egg white, lightly beaten

1 cup/8oz/250g whole almonds in their skins

Method

1. Place all ingredients except the water in a large bowl and allow to stand for 30 minutes to soften the bread and blend the flavors.

2. Purée a third of the mixture at a time in an electric blender or food processor. Pour back into a bowl and thin down to desired consistency with iced water.

3. Cover and chill well. Adjust seasoning to taste. Serve in chilled bowls or in a large bowl over ice.

4. Place garnish ingredients in bowls and hand them separately.

Iced Tomato Soup

Ingredients

3 slices stale bread, crusts removed

4 cups/2¼lb/1kg tomatoes, skinned, seeded and chopped or 2 x 14oz/400g cans tomato, chopped

1 cucumber, peeled, seeded, and chopped

½ cup/4oz/125g minced onions

2 cloves of garlic, crushed

½ green bell pepper, seeded and chopped

1 tsp/5g salt

1 tsp/5g ground cumin

2 tbsp/30ml olive oil

2 tbsp/30ml wine vinegar

2-3 cups/16–24 fl oz/500–750ml iced water

Garnishes

1 red or green bell pepper, diced

1 small cucumber, diced

1 onion, minced

2 hard-boiled eggs, chopped

croûtons

Method

1. Fry the almonds, garlic, parsley, and four slices of the bread in about
4 tbsp/60ml of the oil. When golden, put the contents of the pan in a processor
and liquidize with the cumin, saffron, and a little of the broth. Transfer to a
saucepan, pour in the remaining broth and the milk, season with salt and pepper,
and bring to the boil. Reduce the heat and cook slowly for about 15 minutes.

2. Meanwhile, fry the remaining bread slices in the remaining olive oil until golden
and crisp.

3. Bring the soup to the boil again and add the four slices of fried bread.
Cover, remove from the stove, and leave for 5 minutes before serving.

Almond Soup

Ingredients

1 scant cup/7oz/200g almonds

1 clove of garlic, peeled

1 tbsp/15g finely chopped parsley

8 slices stale bread, preferably brown

⅓ cup/3fl oz/85ml olive oil

1 tsp/5g ground cumin

½ tsp/2.5g saffron

4 cups/ 1¾ pints/1 l chicken broth

1 cup/8 fl oz/250ml milk

salt and pepper

Method

1. Heat the olive oil in a large saucepan and add the carrots, leeks, and bell peppers, and sauté until softened, about 10 minutes. Add the paprika and saffron, continuing to cook for a few minutes more.

2. Add the wine and broth and bring the soup to the boil, simmering for 15 minutes.

3. Add the diced fish, shelled shrimp and squid, and simmer for a further 5 minutes.

4. Garnish with some fresh minced parsley and a squeeze of lemon.

Ingredients

2 tbsp/30ml olive oil

2 large carrots, finely chopped

3 leeks, finely sliced and well washed

1 red bell pepper, chopped

1 green bell pepper, chopped

1 tbsp/15g Spanish paprika or chili pepper

large pinch of saffron threads

Fish Soup with Saffron

2 cups/16 fl oz/500ml white wine

3 cups/24 fl oz/750ml fish broth

14oz/400g firm white fish fillets

1¾ cups/14oz/400g shrimp, shelled and
deveined

1¾ cups/14oz/400g baby calamari

2 tbsp/30g fresh minced parsley

1 lemon, cut into wedges

Spanish

Method

1. Make a superficial cut down the back of each shrimp, then pull out and discard the dark intestinal tract.

2. Heat the oil in a frying pan and stir fry the shrimp for 2-3 minutes until pink. Add the sherry and season with Tabasco sauce, salt, and pepper. Transfer to a dish and serve immediately.

Jumbo Shrimp in Sherry

Ingredients

12 raw jumbo shrimp, peeled

salt and freshly ground black pepper

few drops of Tabasco sauce

2 tbsp/30 ml olive oil

2 tbsp/30 ml sherry

Method

1. Soak the bread in a little water, and squeeze it out before using. The bread also helps to thicken the soup and give it a nice consistency.

2. Blend all the vegetables and the garlic in a food processor, and push it through a sieve into a bowl. Use the mixer to beat the bread, oil, and vinegar together. Add some of the tomato, the cumin seeds, and salt to taste. Add a little water and mix into the bowl with the soup. Add a few ice cubes and refrigerate until thoroughly chilled. You can add more water if necessary.

Gazpacho

Ingredients

2 slices of stale bread

8 cups/4½ lb/2kg tomatoes, washed and roughly chopped

1 cucumber, peeled and chopped

1 green bell pepper, seeded and chopped

1 small onion, peeled and minced

2 cloves of garlic, peeled and minced

5 tbsp/2½ fl oz/75ml olive oil

1-2 tbsp red wine vinegar to taste

1 tsp/5g cumin seeds or powder

Tip

Traditionally the soup was made by crushing the ingredients with a pestle in a mortar and then adding cold water. Gazpacho should be served in wooden bowls and eaten with a wooden spoon, although this isn't always the case! Large quantities of gazpacho can be made at one time as it keeps well—but it won't last long, as you are bound to keep sipping it!

Spanish

Method

1. Preheat the oven to 450°F/230°C and toast the bread slices for 5 minutes. Spread the toast with mayonnaise. Cut the anchovy fillets in pieces to fit on the toast and arrange them on the top. Spread with another layer of mayonnaise and cover with a piece of pimiento the size of the toast. Mix the tomato sauce with the cayenne. Spread 1 tsp/5ml of the tomato sauce on each canapé, sprinkle with the chicken, and garnish with parsley.

Anchovy, Chicken, and Tomato Canapés

Ingredients

10 slices French bread, ¼in/5mm thick

around 1 cup/8 fl oz/250ml mayonnaise

20 anchovy fillets, rinsed to remove excess salt

2 ortega chilies or pimientos

4 tbsp/60ml tomato sauce

dash of cayenne pepper

4 tbsp/60g finely chopped cooked chicken

chopped parsley for garnish

Method

1. Throw the calamari rings in the seasoned flour in a bowl. Whisk the egg and milk together in a bowl. Heat the oil in a heavy-based frying pan.

2. Drop the floured calamari rings, one at a time, into the egg mixture, shaking off any excess liquid. Transfer to the hot oil, in batches if necessary, and fry for 2-3 minutes on each side, or until golden.

3. Drain the fried squid on kitchen paper, then sprinkle with salt. Transfer to a small warmed serving platter and garnish with the lemon wedges.

Ingredients

sea salt

½ cup/4 oz/115g calamari pouches, cut into rings

lemon wedges, to serve

2 tbsp/30 ml seasoned all-purpose flour

1 egg

2 tbsp/30ml milk

olive oil, for frying

Fried Calamari Rings

Spanish

Method

1. Remove the stalks and outer leaves from the artichokes and wash well.
Cut each one into four pieces. Heat the oil in a casserole and gently sauté the
onion and garlic for about 4 minutes. Add the artichokes and wine and season
with salt and nutmeg. Cook gently until done, from 20-40 minutes, depending on
size and type. (Test by pulling on a leaf; if done, it will come away easily.)
If the liquid should reduce too much you can add a little water.

Artichokes Braised in White Wine

Ingredients

6 artichokes

2fl oz/50ml olive oil

1 small onion, peeled and minced

2 cloves of garlic, peeled and thinly sliced

1 scant cup/7fl oz/200ml white wine or dry sherry

salt

freshly grated nutmeg

Method

1. Rinse the peas thoroughly. Place them in a large pot, cover with the water, and bring to the boil. Simmer for 2 minutes then remove from the heat, cover, and let stand for one hour.

2. Meanwhile, heat the oil in a large saucepan and add the paprika, chopped onion, and garlic. Sauté for 5 minutes or until the mixture is fragrant and the onions have softened. Add the green bell pepper, carrot, and diced potato. Toss the vegetables thoroughly with the onion and paprika mixture until well coated, then continue to cook for 10 minutes, stirring thoroughly during the cooking.

3. Add the broth, peas, salt, and pepper to taste then simmer, uncovered, 2-3 hours or until peas are very tender.

4. Cut the kernels off the corn cobs. Reserve ½ cup/4oz/125g of the corn then add the remainder to the soup and simmer for two minutes. Purée the soup until thick and smooth then serve with a few scattered corn kernels and some chopped chives. Garnish each plate with 1 tsp/5ml of low-fat yogurt if desired.

Ingredients

2 cups/1 lb/450g dried green split peas

3 cups/24 fl oz/750ml water

1 tbsp/15ml olive oil

1 tbsp/15g Spanish paprika or chili pepper

2 onions, minced

1 clove of garlic, minced

1 green bell pepper, chopped

Spanish Pea Soup

1 medium carrot, thinly sliced

3 medium red potatoes, peeled and diced

8 cups/3¼ pints/2 l chicken or vegetable broth

salt and pepper to taste

2 ears fresh corn

1 tbsp/15g chopped chives

4 tsp/20ml low fat yogurt to garnish (optional)

Spanish

Method

1. In a large saucepan, combine the broth, bones, garlic head, parsley, salt and pepper. Bring to a boil, reduce heat to medium, and simmer, uncovered, for 30 minutes. Strain into another saucepan. (Makes about 6 cups/48 fl oz/1½ l.)

2. Meanwhile, heat 1 tbsp/15ml oil in a medium frying pan and sauté the chopped garlic over medium heat until lightly golden. Add the ham and cook 1 minute. Stir in the paprika and cumin and remove immediately from heat. Add the garlic mixture to the soup and simmer.

3. Preheat the oven to 350°F/180°C. Arrange bread slices on a cookie sheet and brush lightly on both sides with oil. Bake, turning once, until golden on both sides, about 5 minutes.

4 Place the toasted bread in a soup tureen and pour the hot soup over it. If adding eggs, use an ovenproof tureen, slide them into the soup, and bake at 450°F/230°C until set, about 3 to 4 minutes.

Garlic Soup

Ingredients

7 cups/56 fl oz/1¾ l chicken broth

2 beef bones

1 head garlic, separated into cloves, unpeeled,

8 cloves of garlic, peeled and chopped

4 parsley sprigs

salt and freshly ground pepper

2½–3 tbsp/40–45ml olive oil

¼ lb/115g cured ham, such as prosciutto, sliced

¼ in/¼ cm thick and diced

1 tbsp/15g paprika

½ tsp/2.5g ground cumin

8 slices French bread, ¼in/5mm thick

4 large eggs (optional)

Spanish

Method

1. To make the sauce, gently fry the onion and carrot in the oil.
Add the tomato purée, parsley, and flour. Stir well and cook for a minute
then add the white wine, cold water, and some salt and pepper.
Bring to the boil, reduce the heat, cover, and cook slowly whilst you prepare
the stuffing.

2. Heat the oil in a frying pan then add the onion, garlic, and parsley and
sauté for a few minutes. Next add the ground meat. Mix the ingredients
well and cook for a few minutes. Squeeze the fresh breadcrumbs dry,
season with salt and pepper, add to the mixture, and cook for another
4 minutes, stirring constantly. Preheat the oven to 375°F/190°C.

3. Stuff the bell peppers with the mixture and put them in an ovenproof
dish. Sieve the sauce or purée it in a liquidizer. Pour into the dish and bake
for half an hour.

Ingredients

8 medium-sized red, yellow, and green bell peppers

salt and pepper

Sauce

1 onion, peeled and finely chopped

1 carrot, scraped and chopped

3 tbsp/45ml olive oil

1 tbsp/15ml tomato purée

1 tsp/5g chopped parsley

1 tbsp/15g all-purpose (plain) flour

Stuffed Peppers (Chiles rellenos)

5fl oz/145ml white wine

3 ½ fl oz/100ml water

Stuffing

4 tbsp/60ml olive oil

1 onion, peeled and finely chopped

1 clove of garlic, peeled and finely chopped

2 tsp/10g chopped parsley

1 heaping cup/9oz/255g ground pork, beef, or lamb

5 tbsp/2¼oz/65g fresh bread crumbs, soaked in a little milk

Spanish

31

Method

1. Using a small sharp knife, cut off woody end of asparagus stems. Working from tip to bottom, scrape off scales from stems. Tie stems into 4 bundles with kitchen string.

2. In a deep saucepan, bring 2in/5cm of water to a boil. Add asparagus bundles, tips pointing upward. Cover pan with a lid or dome of foil and simmer 8 to 10 minutes or until asparagus is just tender. Remove asparagus and untie bundles. Drain asparagus on a thick wad of paper towels. Arrange on a warmed serving platter, and sprinkle the egg over stems. Cover and keep warm.

3. Meanwhile, heat the oil in a frying pal. Add garlic and sauté until lightly browned. Discard garlic. Stir the bread crumbs into the pan and cook 5–7 minutes, stirring, until crisp and golden. Remove from heat and stir in parsley, then pour it over the asparagus, leaving tips uncovered. Serve immediately.

Asparagus with Egg

Ingredients

1½ lb/680g fresh asparagus

1 hard-boiled egg, finely chopped

⅓ cup/3½ fl oz/100ml olive oil

1 clove of garlic

¾ cup fresh, coarse bread crumbs

2 tbsp/30g chopped fresh parsley

Method

1. Wash the fish then sprinkle with salt inside and out. Preheat the oven to 400°F/200°C. Put the fish in a large, oval ovenproof dish. Cut two slices of the onion in half and fit them into one of the slits in the fish; do the same with two slices of the tomato and the lemon in the other slits. Put some lemon inside the fish and some parsley and place a round of lemon in the eye. Pour the oil over the fish. Arrange the potato slices around the dish and any remaining slices of onion and tomato. Season and transfer to the oven.

2. Bake for about 20-25 minutes. If the fish is large, cover the top with a piece of foil for about 15 minutes of the cooking time. Baste occasionally. If you are not going to serve immediately, turn off the oven 10 minutes before the fish has finished cooking, leaving it inside. The fish will be done but not overcooked.

Ingredients

1 whole sea bream, about 3¼ lb/1½ kg in weight

salt

1 onion, peeled and sliced

2 tomatoes, washed and sliced

1 lemon, washed and sliced

sprig of parsley

⅔ cup/5fl oz/145ml olive oil

4 medium potatoes, peeled and thinly sliced

Baked Sea Bream

Spanish

Method

1. Cover the beans with cold water and soak overnight. Drain and rinse.

2. In a large soup pot, combine beans with the water, chorizo, salt pork, onion, garlic, parsley, bayleaf, pepper, and cumin. In a small cup, mix together the oil and paprika until smooth, and stir into the pot. Bring to a boil, cover and simmer about 2 hours, or until beans are tender. Add salt to taste. Turn off the heat and let stand 20 minutes to thicken, then reheat. Serve in soup bowls, being sure to add a piece of chorizo and salt pork to each serving.

Bean Stew with Chorizo

Ingredients

2 cups/1lb/455g dried white haricot or navy
beans

5 cups/2 pints/1¼ l water

4oz/115g chorizo, sliced

4oz/115g salt pork or slab bacon, cut in

1in/2½cm cubes

1 small onion, chopped

4 cloves of garlic

2 tbsp/30g minced parsley

1 bayleaf

freshly ground pepper

¼ tsp/1.25g ground cumin

1 tbsp/15ml olive oil

1 tsp/5g paprika or chili pepper

salt

Spanish

Method

1. Cover the chickpeas with cold water and soak overnight.

2. In a large soup pot, combine the water, beef, chicken, salt pork, ham, beef bone, salt, and pepper. Bring to a boil, cover and simmer for 1½ hours. Let cool and refrigerate overnight if you wish to remove the fat that solidifies on the surface.

3. Drain and rinse chickpeas. Add to soup pot (preferably in a loose piece of cheesecloth (muslin) to keep them together) with the chorizo, carrot, whole garlic, turnip, leek, whole onion, parsley, and saffron. Bring to a boil, cover and simmer about 2 hours, or until chickpeas are almost tender. Add potatoes and cook 30 minutes more. Taste and adjust the seasoning.

4. Meanwhile, prepare the cabbage. Heat the oil in a large frying pan and sauté the minced garlic and chopped onion over medium-high heat until onion is wilted. Add cabbage, season with salt and pepper, and stir-fry 5 minutes. Cover, reduce the heat, and cook 5 minutes more. Cook the fideos noodles or vermicelli in a separate pan of boiling salted water until just done; drain.

5. To serve, strain the broth, returning enough of it to the pot to keep the remaining ingredients moist. Combine broth with noodles and serve as a first course.

6. Cut meats and vegetables into serving pieces. Arrange with cabbage on 1 or 2 large platters with the chickpeas heaped in the center.

Ingredients

1½ cups/12oz/350g dried chickpeas (garbanzo beans)

12 cups/5¼ pints/3 l water

1lb/455g lean beef, cubed

1lb/455g large chicken thighs

4oz/115g salt pork or slab bacon

4oz/115g cured ham, such as prosciutto, in a thick slice

1 beef bone

salt and freshly ground pepper

4oz/115g chorizo sausage or other mild or breakfast sausage

Madrid Boiled Dinner
(Cocida madrileña)

1 large carrot

2 large whole cloves of garlic plus 1 clove, minced

1 turnip, halved

1 large leek, washed and trimmed

1 small whole onion plus 3 tbsp/45g chopped onion

2 parsley sprigs

few threads saffron

6 small red potatoes, unpeeled

2 tbsp/30ml olive oil

1 small green cabbage, coarsely chopped

3oz/85g fideos or vermicelli

Spanish

39

Method

1. Boil the cauliflower in lightly salted water, being careful not to overcook it. Drain off the water and break into flowerets.

2. Heat the garlic in the oil. Dry the cauliflower in a clean towel and sauté in the oil and garlic until golden. Season with salt and pepper and sprinkle with parsley.

Cauliflower Sautéed in Garlic

Ingredients

1 medium cauliflower

2 cloves of garlic, peeled and sliced

⅓ cup/3½ fl oz/100ml olive oil

salt and white pepper

1 tsp/5g chopped parsley

Method

1. Put the olives in a small bowl, cover with warm water, and set aside.

2. Preheat the oven to 350°F/180°C. Sprinkle the duck inside and out with salt and pepper. Truss the duck, place it in a roasting pan, and prick it all over with a fork. Roast for 1 hour.

3. Meanwhile, heat the oil in a shallow flameproof Dutch oven (casserole) and sauté the onion, carrots, and garlic over medium-high heat until onion is wilted.

4. Remove the backbone and rib cage from the duck and discard them. Cut the duck into serving pieces and transfer them to the Dutch oven (casserole). Pour off the fat in the roasting pan and deglaze the pan with the broth, scraping up any particles stuck to the bottom. Strain the liquid into the Dutch oven (casserole).

5. Drain the olives. Add them to the Dutch oven (casserole) with the sherry, thyme, parsley, salt, and pepper. Bring to a boil on top of the stove, cover, then cook in the oven 1 hour.

Duck with Olives and Sherry

Ingredients

½ cup/4oz/125g sliced or chopped large Spanish green olives

5lb/2¼kg duck, as much fat removed as possible

salt and freshly ground pepper

1 tbsp/15ml olive oil

1 medium onion, finely chopped

2 carrots, finely chopped

3 cloves of garlic, minced

¾ cup/6fl oz chicken broth

¼ cup/2fl oz dry sherry or white wine

¼ tsp/1.25g dried thyme

1 tbsp/15g minced parsley

Method

1. Sift flour and salt into a bowl. Stir in yeast.

2. Stir the milk into the egg yolk, then slowly pour into flour, stirring constantly. Beat 5 to 10 minutes, or until dough comes cleanly away from bowl.

3. Turn dough onto a lightly floured surface and knead until smooth and elastic. Form into a ball, place in an oiled bowl, cover, and leave in a warm place about 1 hour until doubled in bulk.

4. Meanwhile, heat 3 tbsp/45ml of the oil in a skillet. Add onions, bell pepper, and herbs and cook over medium heat, stirring occasionally, 20 to 25 minutes or until vegetables are soft but not browned. Add 2–3 tbsp/30–45ml water if necessary to prevent browning. Season with salt and pepper and set aside.

5. Preheat oven to 450°F/230°C. On a lightly floured surface, punch down and flatten dough. Roll out to a 12-inch/30cm circle. Carefully transfer to an oiled cookie sheet and turn up the edge to make a rim. Prick well with a fork.

6. Spread vegetable mixture over dough, arrange anchovy fillets on top, drizzle with remaining oil, and bake 25 to 30 minutes or until the dough is well risen, crisp, and golden. Serve warm.

Ingredients

2 cups/250g/8oz all-purpose (strong, plain) flour

salt and pepper

1 tsp/5g active dry yeast

⅔ cup/6fl oz/175ml warm milk

1 egg yolk

4 tbsp/60ml olive oil

Bell Pepper & Onion Tart

2 cups/18oz/500g Spanish (Bermuda) onions, halved and sliced

4 red bell peppers, sliced

4 yellow bell peppers, sliced

about ½ cup/2oz/50g mixed fresh thyme, oregano
and parsley sprigs

16-20 canned anchovy fillets, drained

Method

1. Pat chicken pieces dry with kitchen paper and sprinkle with a few grindings of pepper.

2. Heat oil over a moderate heat in a heavy pan. Add diced salt pork or pancetta and cook stirring until brown and crisp. Remove pork with a slotted spoon and drain on paper towels.

3. Add chicken to fat in pan and brown evenly on all sides. Set chicken aside.

4. Pour off all but a little fat from pan. Stir in onions and garlic and cook for about 5 minutes until onions are soft and transparent. Stir in paprika, then tomato and bring to boil, stirring frequently. Cook briskly, uncovered, about 5 minutes until most of liquid in pan has evaporated.

5. Return chicken and pork to pan, add rice, peas, boiling water and saffron or turmeric, stir well to combine. Bring quickly to boil and reduce heat to low, cover and simmer for 20-30 minutes until chicken and rice are tender and all liquid is absorbed. Taste and adjust seasoning. Sprinkle with parsley and serve.

Ingredients

3lb/1½kg roasting chicken, cut into 6-8 serving pieces

freshly ground black pepper

2 tbsp/30ml oil

4oz/115g salt pork, or pancetta, finely diced

2 sliced Spanish (Bermuda) onions

1 tsp/5g minced garlic

2½ tsp/12.5g paprika or chili pepper

Chicken with Saffron Rice & Peas

1 medium sized tomato, finely chopped

1¼ cups/10oz/280g uncooked rice

⅔ cup/5oz/145g fresh or frozen peas

3 cups/24 fl oz/750ml boiling water

⅛ tsp/2g ground saffron or

1 tsp/5g turmeric

2 tbsp/30g minced parsley

Spanish

Method

1. Heat the oil in a heavy-based frying pan. Add the lamb and cook, stirring occasionally, until lightly browned. Do this in batches if necessary so the pieces are not crowded. Using a slotted spoon, transfer meat to a plate or bowl and reserve.

2. Stir onion into pan and cook about 5 minutes, stirring occasionally, until softened. Stir in garlic and cook 2 minutes, then stir in paprika. When well blended, stir in lamb and any juices on plate or in bowl, the parsley, lemon juice, salt, and pepper. Cover tightly and cook over very low heat 1¼–1½ hours, shaking pan occasionally, until lamb is very tender. If necessary, add 3 tbsp/45ml wine or water.

Lamb with Lemon & Garlic

Ingredients

3 tbsp/45ml olive oil

2lb/740g lean, boneless lamb, cut into

1in/2½cm pieces

1 Spanish (Bermuda) onion, finely chopped

3 cloves of garlic, crushed

1 tbsp/15g paprika

3 tbsp/45g finely chopped fresh parsley

3 tbsp/45ml fresh lemon juice

salt and pepper

3 tbsp/45ml dry white wine or water (optional)

Method

In a frying pan, saute the sliced mushrooms in oil and butter, adding

a pinch of salt and black pepper. Set aside. In the same pan, fry the

bread on both sides, until golden, arrange on serving dishes,

and keep hot. In the same pan, fry the fillets of beef, seasoning if

desired, and place on top of the slices of bread. In the remaining oil,

toss the pieces of ham, truffle, and liver. Stir well and add the

tomato paste and sherry, leaving to heat through for one minute.

To serve, pour the sauce over the fillets and arrange the mushrooms

on the side. Serve very hot.

Ingredients

4 x 5½oz/150g fillets of beef

2 oz/50g serrano ham, diced

4 slices white bread, thinly sliced

1 chicken liver, cut into small pieces

1 black truffle, sliced or cut into small pieces

1 small glass of dry sherry

Fillet Steak with Mushrooms

1 tbsp tomato paste

2 cups/8oz/50g mushrooms, washed and thinly sliced

olive oil

butter

salt and black pepper

Spanish

Method

1. Sprinkle chicken with salt. Heat the oil in a shallow flameproof casserole and brown the chicken over medium-high heat on all sides. Add the chopped garlic, reduce heat to medium, and cook, stirring occasionally, for 30 minutes. Stir in the minced garlic, parsley, and wine. Cover and cook for 15 minutes more, or until chicken is done and the juices run clear when the thigh is pricked with a fork.

Ingredients

3 ½ lb/1 ½ kg chicken, cut in small serving pieces

(split the breast and cut in half again; cut each

thigh in half)

salt

5 tbsp olive oil

6 cloves of garlic, chopped, plus 1 clove, minced

1 tbsp minced parsley

2 tbsp dry white wine

Chicken in Garlic Sauce

Spanish

Method

1. Combine the pork, parsley, garlic, onion, bread crumbs, half the beaten egg, salt, and pepper. Form into 1in/2½cm balls, then roll them in flour.

2. Pour oil into a frying pan, until it is at least ½in/1cm deep, and heat until a cube of bread browns in 60 seconds. Dip the meatballs in the remaining beaten egg and place directly in the hot oil. Lower the flame and fry slowly until well browned on both sides and cooked through.

Aioli Sauce

1. Crush the garlic in a mortar with salt until it becomes a pulp then gradually beat in the oil. The result should be sort of pale thick mayonnaise. The milder sort is made exactly like mayonnaise; simply crush the garlic with the lemon juice and egg yolk and then add the salt and oil.

Makes 1 cup/8fl oz/250ml

Pork Meatballs with Aioli

Ingredients

1 cup/8oz/225g ground pork loin

7 tbsp/ minced parsley

2 cloves of garlic, minced

1 tbsp minced onion

3 tbsp/45g fresh bread crumbs

2 eggs, lightly beaten

salt

freshly ground pepper

flour for dusting

oil for frying

Aioli Sauce

4 cloves of garlic, peeled and minced

1 tsp/5g salt

1 cup/8fl oz/250ml olive oil

Method

1. Heat butter and oil together in a large pan. Fry potatoes until tender and browned on both sides. Drain on kitchen paper. Place on serving platter and sprinkle with salt, pepper, and chopped parsley.

Spanish Fried Potatoes

Ingredients

1½ tbsp/¾ oz butter

3 tbsp/45ml olive oil

4 potatoes, peeled and sliced ¾ in/7½mm thick

salt and pepper

chopped parsley

Spanish

Method

Start by slicing the fillets nearly all the way through the center, opening them like a book. Leave to soak in the milk for 2 hours. Drain them well, season with pepper, and with salt if necessary, remembering that the ham is already salted.

Now fill the fillets by placing in each first a slice of serrano ham, then a slice of pimento, a small piece of lard or butter and a ring of hard-boiled egg. Roll up the fillets, securing them with a cocktail stick or kitchen twine.

Have the beaten egg ready in a shallow bowl. Dip the fillets in it, then roll them in the bread crumbs in a separate dish. In a large frying pan, heat the oil and fry the fillet rolls until golden brown.

A bowl of hot tomato sauce goes well with this dish.

Ingredients

8 pork fillets, about 1 inch/2cm thick

1¼cups/10fl oz/300ml milk

8 thin slices of serrano or country ham

⅓ cup/3½oz/100g lard or butter

4 canned red pimentos, cut in half lengthwise

Rolled Pork Fillets (Flamenquillos)

1 hard boiled egg, sliced

1 beaten egg

dried bread crumbs

olive oil for frying

Method

1. Mix together the garlic, lime rind, half the lime juice, 2 tbsp of the oil, and 1 tbsp of the rosemary in a large bowl. Add the tuna and turn to coat evenly. Cover and place in the fridge for 30 minutes to marinate.

2. Preheat the oven to 425°F/220°C. Place the tomatoes and onion in a shallow ovenproof dish with the remaining rosemary. Drizzle with the remaining oil and season. Bake for 15-20 minutes, or until tender and lightly browned.

3. Lightly oil a ridged cast-iron grill pan or large frying pan and heat over a fairly high heat.

Add the tuna and cook for 4-5 minutes on each side until golden. Serve with the tomatoes and onion, sprinkled with the remaining lime juice.

Seared Tuna with Roasted Plum Tomatoes

Ingredients

1 clove of garlic, minced

1 lime, rind grated, juice squeezed

5 tbsp/75ml olive oil, plus extra for greasing

3 tbsp/45g chopped fresh rosemary

4 tuna steaks, about 5oz/145g each, about ¾ in/2cm thick

6 plum tomatoes, halved lengthwise

1 red onion, halved and thinly sliced lengthwise

salt and black pepper

Spanish

Method

Wash and dry the fish. Season on both sides with salt. Heat the broiler or grill.
Put the fish on a grill pan, the sort that has a drip-tray for catching the juices,
and pour half the oil over each slice. Next, sprinkle a mixture of half the garlic and
parsley over the fish. Squeeze a few drops of lemon juice over it, and place under
a hot broiler or over the grill. When the slices are golden (about 5 minutes)
turn them over and repeat the operation.

When the fish is cooked serve it in a warmed dish and pour the juices from the
pan over it. It can be served with mayonnaise.

Ingredients

1lb/5oz/600g swordfish steaks

salt

4 tbsp/60ml olive oil

2 cloves of garlic, peeled and minced

2 tbsp/30ml minced parsley

1 lemon, juice squeezed

Grilled Swordfish

Method

1. With a sharp knife, remove membrane from the kidneys. Cut each kidney in half lengthwise, then snip out and discard cores. Quarter kidneys, then set aside.

2. Heat the oil in a frying pan. Add garlic and cook 2 to 3 minutes. Stir in mushrooms and ham and fry until liquid from mushrooms has evaporated.

3. Stir kidneys into pan and fry 2 to 3 minutes, stirring frequently, so kidneys are lightly browned on outside and still pink in center. Add seasoning and sherry and boil, stirring occasionally, until sherry has almost evaporated. Garnish with parsley and serve hot.

Ingredients

1lb/455g lamb kidneys

3 tbsp/45ml olive oil

2 cloves of garlic, minced

2 cups/8oz/250g chopped mushrooms

2oz/55g serrano or country ham, sliced

salt and pepper

6-8 tbsp fino sherry

fresh parsley to garnish

Kidneys in Sherry

Method

1. In a shallow bowl, mix together the oil, minced garlic, parsley, thyme, and lemon juice. Add the chops and coat well. Cover and refrigerate for at least 2 hours.

2. To make the Quick Aioli, whisk together all the ingredients in a small bowl.

3. Transfer to a serving bowl.

4. Drain the chops, reserving the marinade. Cook the chops under a preheated broiler or over a hot charcoal grill until browned and done to taste, basting occasionally with the marinade. Season with salt and pepper. Serve with the aioli.

Ingredients

6 tbsp/90ml olive oil

2 cloves of garlic, minced

2 tbsp/30g minced parsley

1 tbsp/15g chopped fresh thyme or ½ tsp/2,5g dried thyme

1½ tbsp/20ml lemon juice

12 rib lamb chops, each ¾ in/2cm thick

salt and freshly ground pepper

Lamb Chops with Garlic Mayonnaise

Quick Aioli

¾ cup/6fl oz/175ml mayonnaise

1 tbsp/15ml extra-virgin olive oil

4 cloves of garlic, or to taste, mashed through a garlic press

1 tbsp/15ml lemon juice

Method

1. Preheat oven to moderate temperature 350°F/180°C.

2. Lightly brush a shallow ovenproof dish with olive oil and arrange fish in it.

Brush the top of each fish steak with olive oil.

3. Combine parsley, garlic, almonds, shallots, paprika, lemon rind, and

1½ tbsp/20ml olive oil. Spoon over fish, and press down well.

4. Bake fish in a moderate oven for 10 minutes.

5. Pour the tomatoes around the fish, and cook for a further 10 minutes.

Spanish-Style Fish Steaks

Ingredients

4 sea-bass or grouper steaks	1 tbsp/15g chopped shallots
olive oil	½ tsp/2.5g ground paprika or mild chili pepper
1 tbsp/15g dried parsley flakes	½ tsp/2.5g grated lemon rind
3 tsp/15g freshly crushed garlic	15oz/425g can tomatoes, drained and
2 tbsp/1oz/30g almonds (slivered)	roughly chopped

Method

1. Prepare fish; cut off fins and remove backbone. Leave on head and tail and wipe over with damp kitchen paper. Preheat the oven to 350°F/180°C. Arrange fish in a shallow ovenproof dish, cover with onion rings, carrots, and parsley.

2. Add remaining ingredients, cover with lid or foil, and bake for 25 minutes.

3. Allow to cool completely before serving. Serve as an appetizer or an hors d'oeuvre.

Ingredients

1½lb/750g fresh sardines

2 onions, sliced into thin rings

1 carrot, thinly sliced

1 tbsp/15g chopped parsley

½ cup/4 fl oz/125ml white wine vinegar

½ cup/4 fl oz/125ml water

Marinated Sardines

¼ tsp/1.25g ground cinnamon

1 bayleaf

6 peppercorns

½ tsp/2.5g dried thyme

½ tsp/2.5g salt

2 tbsp/30ml olive oil

Spanish

Method

1. Cut off the fish heads, pulling out their innards. Slit them down the belly, as far as the tail, and rinse the insides under a faucet. Then put each fish down on a board, black back upward, and press a thumb firmly down on it. This opens it out like a book and makes it easy to rip out the backbone and tail.

Heat 4 tbsp of oil in a large frying pan. Dust the fish with seasoned flour on a cookie sheet and fry as soon as you have a trayful (about four fish). Lay them in skin side down first and turn after 1 to 2 minutes. Drain on kitchen paper. Take the pan off the heat between batches and add more oil as necessary. Fry the garlic in the remaining oil, then transfer it to a mortar or a small herb or coffee grinder. Work to a paste with a pinch of salt, the saffron, cumin seeds, and ginger. Work in the vinegar. Arrange the fish in an earthenware dish, skin side upward. The dish should be shallow if you are planning to serve the fish within 24 hours, but should be smaller and deeper if you want to keep them.

2. Mix 1 cup/8fl oz/250ml of water into the spice mixture and pour this over the fish. Add more vinegar and water to cover completely if you are keeping them. Arrange the bayleaves and very thinly sliced lemon over the top. Refrigerate for half a day before eating. They can be served straight from the dish and should be eaten within a week.

Ingredients

2¼lb/1kg small fish (fresh anchovies, sardines, whitebait, etc.)

6-8 tbsp/90–110ml olive oil

4 tbsp/2 oz/55g all-purpose flour

salt and freshly ground black pepper

6 cloves of garlic, minced

small pinch of saffron strands

Moorish Pickled Fish

1 tsp/5g cumin seeds

1 tsp/5g ground ginger

1 cup/8fl oz/250ml red wine vinegar

4 bayleaves

1 lemon, thinly sliced

73

Method:

1. Season chicken thighs with salt, freshly ground black pepper, and paprika. Heat oil in frying pan and cook chicken until golden brown on both sides. Reduce heat and cover chicken with water, white wine, bayleaf, and simmer for around 15minutes. Remove chicken and reserve the cooking liquid.

2. To the same pan add Spanish sausage and cook for 4minutes. Then add calamari, peppers, tomato, onion, and saffron. Stir, cover, and cook over gentle heat stirring occasionally for 10 minutes. Sprinkle the rice over the cooked vegetables in pan and pour over 1½ cups/12fl oz/350ml of the cooking liquid. Bring to the boil, reduce the heat, cover and simmer for 20 minutes, stirring occasionally.

3. Place shrimp, chicken, and mussels on top of rice mixture. Check rice and add more liquid if required. Cover and cook over gentle heat until rice is tender and shrimp and mussels are cooked. Discard any mussels that have not opened. Serve with lemon and lime wedges and fresh country bread direct to the table from the pan.

Ingredients:

2 green peppers halved, deseeded, and cut into lengthwise strips

4 fresh or canned tomatoes, peeled, seeded, and chopped

1 medium onion, minced

250g/8oz calamari pouches, cleaned, rinsed, and cut into rings

2 cups/500g medium-large green shrimp

10½oz/300g fresh mussels, scrubbed and cleaned

4-6 chicken thighs

4oz/125g chorizo or pepperoni, sliced diagonally

Paella Valenciana

salt and freshly ground black pepper to taste

½ tsp/2.5g paprika

3 tbsp/45ml oil for frying

1½ cups/12fl oz/350ml water

1 cup/8fl oz/ dry white wine

1 bayleaf

pinch saffron threads

⅔ cup/5oz/150g long grain rice

heavy based pan or paella pan

Method

1. With a sharp knife, cut the pork rind into strips about ½ in/1 cm wide and 1 in/2½cm long.

 2. Pour vegetable oil into a deep heavy-based frying pan to a depth of 1 in/2½cm. Heat the oil until a cube of bread browns in 1 minute. Cook the strips of rind in the oil for 1-2 minutes, until puffed up and golden. Bleed dry on kitchen paper and sprinkle with paprika and salt to taste. Serve hot or cold. The rinds can be stored in an airtight container for up to 2 weeks.

Ingredients

sea salt

paprika

4 oz/115g pork rind

vegetable oil, for frying

Pork Cracklings (Chicharones)

Tip

Provided that the rinds are kept in a closed,

airtight container, it keeps up tp 2 weeks.

The are delicious as snacks, eaten the Mexican

way, sprinkled with chili pepper and lime juice.

Spanish

77

Method

1. Sprinkle the pork with salt and leave for about an hour. Preheat the oven to 440°F/200°C.

2. Rub the meat with the butter, and season it with nutmeg and pepper. Brown in a frying pan on all sides, then flame with the brandy. Place the meat on a low rack, or upturned plate, in a fairly deep dish that will hold the meat snugly, cover with milk and cook in the oven for about 90 minutes. You can also cook it on top of the stove over a low flame if you prefer. After about an hour, add the walnuts. Adjust the seasoning and add more milk if necessary.

3. When the meat is cooked, remove it, slice it, and serve the sauce separately. Mashed potato and applesauce are the best accompaniments. Just slice the apples and bake them with a little butter, salt, a few drops of lemon juice, and a pinch of cinnamon.

Ingredients

3½ lb/1½ kg lean pork (boneless weight)

coarse salt and freshly ground black pepper

1 tbsp/15g butter

freshly grated nutmeg

1 tbsp/15ml brandy

4 cups/1¾ pints/1 l milk

⅔ cup/5oz/145g shelled walnuts, scalded and peeled if desired

Pork in Walnut Sauce

Spanish

Tip

Baked apple slices are also a good accompaniment. Just slice the apples and bake them with a little butter, salt, a few drops of lemon juice, and a pinch of cinnamon.

Method

1. Preheat the oven to 375°F/190°C. Rub the Cornish hens (poussins) with salt and pepper (inside and out). Brush the skins with the olive oil, and stuff a lemon wedge, and bayleaf inside each one. Roast these for about 45 minutes, until tender.

2. Meanwhile, heat the olive oil in a large frying pan, and sauté the onion and garlic until translucent. Add the tomatoes and fry lightly for a further 2 minutes. Add all the remaining ingredients and simmer for 20-25 minutes, until the sauce has thickened and the tomatoes are soft.

3. Place the Cornish hens (poussins) on a serving dish and spoon over the sauce. Serve with remaining sauce in a jug.

Ingredients

4 small Cornish hens (poussins)

salt and freshly ground black pepper

olive oil to brush

4 small lemon wedges

4 bayleaves

2 tbsp olive oil

1 medium onion, thinly sliced

3 cloves of garlic, crushed

1lb/455g tomatoes, skinned, seeded, and roughly chopped

Poussins with Almonds and Pine Nuts

½ cup/4fl oz/125ml red wine

2 tbsp/30g sun-dried tomato purée

1 green chili pepper, deseeded and thinly sliced

1 medium red bell pepper, cut into thin strips

1 small green bell pepper, cut into thin strips

3 tbsp/45g blanched almonds, chopped

1 tbsp/15g pine nuts

12 pitted black olives

2 tbsp/50g raisins

Method

1. Soak raisins in cold water for 15 minutes. Drain well.

2. Cut off roots from spinach just above the pink tip and wash in 3 changes of water. Shake off excess water and place in a large saucepan. Cover and cook over medium heat until spinach has just wilted. Remove to a colander to cool and drain. Chop spinach roughly.

3. In a large frying pan, heat 1 tbsp/15ml oil, add pine nuts and cook while stirring until golden. Remove with a slotted spoon. Add remaining tablespoon/15ml of oil, onion and garlic, and cook over moderate heat until onion is soft but not colored.

4. Add spinach, drained raisins, salt and pepper, and toss gently to heat through. Sprinkle over the pine nuts. Serve hot as a side dish.

Ingredients

3 tbsp/45g raisins

2 cups/4oz/125g spinach

2 tbsp/30ml olive oil

2 tbsp/30g pine nuts

1 medium onion, finely chopped

1 clove of garlic, crushed

salt and freshly ground black pepper

Spinach with Raisins and Pine Nuts

Spanish

Method

Warm the cooked rice. Heat the oil over medium heat in a large frying pan and add the onions. Cook, stirring, about 5 minutes. Add the garlic and cook another minute. Add the peppers and tomatoes, cover, and cook about 5 minutes. Add the rice, mix, replace the cover, and cook another minute or so. Taste for salt and pepper and serve immediately.

Ingredients

3 cups/1lb 10oz/750g cooked rice

3 tbsp/45ml olive oil

1 medium onion, finely diced

1 tbsp/15g minced garlic

1 small green bell pepper, finely diced

1 small red bell pepper, finely diced

2 ripe tomatoes, skinned, seeded, and diced

salt and pepper to taste

Spanish Rice

Method

1. In a saucepan, bring the water, milk, 5 tbsp/75ml oil, salt, and lemon rind to a boil. Add the flour all at once, reduce the heat, and stir vigorously with a wooden spoon until dough leaves the sides of the pan and forms a smooth ball. Cook, turning the dough frequently for 2 to 3 minutes. Remove from heat and cool slightly.

2. In a food processor process dough 20 seconds. Add eggs and process for another 30 seconds.

3. Heat about 1in/2½cm oil to 375°F/190°C in a large frying pan or electric fryer. Drop teaspoons of dough into hot oil. The dough should puff up, forming fritters, becoming golden and hollow inside. Using a slotted spoon, remove fritters from the pan and drain on paper towels. Dust with sugar before serving.

Light-as-the-Wind Fritters

Ingredients

½ cup/4 fl oz/125ml water

½ cup/4 fl oz/125ml milk

5 tbsp/75ml olive oil plus additional oil

for deep frying

¼ tsp/1.25g salt

¼ tsp/1.25g grated lemon rind

1 cup/4oz/125g all-purpose (plain) flour

4 large eggs

powdered sugar for dusting

Method

Heat the oven to 300°F/150°C.

In a bowl, beat the eggs, sugar, grated lemon rind, and cinnamon until thick and creamy. Carefully stir in the ground almonds. Butter a circular baking tin or bundt pan and grease well with the butter, then dust with flour. Pour in the mixture and bake for about 30 minutes. Leave to cool before removing from the pan and placing on a round serving platter. Dust with the powdered sugar.

Ingredients

4 large eggs

1 scant cup/7oz/200g sugar

1 scant cup/7 oz/200g ground almonds

1 tsp/5g ground cinnamon

1 lemon, rind grated

2 tbsp/1oz/25g butter

2 tbsp/1oz/25g all-purpose flour

4 tbsp/50g powdered sugar

Santiago Almond Tart

Spanish

Method

1. Beat the egg yolks with the sugar. In a saucepan, heat the cream to boiling point and stir into the egg and sugar mixture. Return it all to the saucepan in which you have heated the cream and stir until it boils. Flavor with cherry liqueur. Pour the cream over the fruit and place under the broiler for a few seconds.

Fruit Gratin

Ingredients

8 egg yolks

1 cup/8oz/250g sugar

3 cups/24 fl oz/750ml light (single) cream

1 tsp/5ml cherry liqueur

5 cups/2¼ lb/1kg prepared mixed fresh fruit

Method

1. Bring the milk to the boil in two or more saucepans. Let it cool.

2. Put the butter in a very large saucepan (not aluminum) over a gentle heat. When it starts to soften, brush the butter up the sides, then add the boiled cooked milk, rice, salt, and cinnamon sticks. Bring to the boil, then lower the heat and cook gently, stirring frequently with a wooden spoon until it is done. It will take about 2 hours.

3. Just before the rice is ready, stir in the sugar. Leave the pudding to rest for about 10 minutes before serving sprinkled with cinnamon. Well worth the time and trouble!

Rice Pudding

Ingredients

5 quarts/9 pints/5 l milk

½ cup/4½ oz/125g butter

2 cups/1 lb/500g Spanish short-grain rice

1 tsp/5ml salt

2 cinnamon sticks

2 cups/1 lb/500g sugar

powdered cinnamon

Method

1. To caramelize sugar, in a small heavy saucepan, cook the superfine (caster) sugar and water over medium heat, stirring constantly, until the syrup turns golden in color (the sugar will crystallise before it liquifies). Immediately pour the syrup into 6 individual custard cups.

2. Preheat the oven to 350°F/175°C. Whisk the whole eggs and egg yolks in a large bowl until uniform in color. Whisk in the milk, sugar, salt, and lemon zest. Divide the mixture among the prepared cups. Place cups in a baking pan and add enough hot water to come halfway up their sides. Bake about 45 minutes, or until a knife inserted in the custard comes out clean. Remove cups from pan and let cool. Cover and refrigerate until chilled.

3. Run a knife around the edge of each cup and unmold the flan, spooning the caramelized sugar over it. Serve with the whipped cream, if desired.

Caramel Custard

Ingredients

½ cup/4oz/125g superfine (caster) sugar

2 tbsp/30 ml water

3 whole eggs

2 egg yolks

2½ cups/1 pint/600 ml milk

6 tbsp/6 oz/175g sugar

pinch of salt

¼ tsp/1.25g grated lemon rind

whipped cream, if desired

Index